Wealthy SPEAKER

Workbook and Planning Guide

The **Proven Formula**
for building your
successful speaking business

Jane Atkinson

© 2006, Jane Atkinson

All rights reserved. No part of this publication may be reproduced, transmitted or stored in any form or by any means without the prior written permission of the author.

The material in this publication is provided for information purposes only. Procedures, laws and regulations are constantly changing and the examples given are intended to be general guidelines only. This book is sold with the understanding that no one involved in this publication is attempting herein to render professional advice.

ISBN 0-9780059-1-0
First Printing

Atkinson, Jane, 1964-
Wealthy speaker. Workbook and planning guide / Jane Atkinson.

ISBN 0-9780059-1-0

1. Public speaking—Problems, exercises, etc. 2. Public speaking—Vocational guidance. I. Title.

PN4098.A85 2006 Suppl. 808.5'1'023 C2006-900100-6

Editor: **Catherine Leek of Green Onion Publishing**
Back Cover and Interior Design,
Electronic Page Composition: **Heidy Lawrance Associates**
Front Cover Design: **Tim Handleman**
Cartoons: **Steve Morris**

CONTENTS

TO MY READERS

Dear Speaker,

Welcome to the *Wealthy Speaker Workbook and Planning Guide*, an *essential* component of The Wealthy Speaker System. This workbook is designed to help you walk through the Wealthy Speaker process and I've thrown in some bonus questions and quizzes to help lock in the learning.

If you follow the Ready, Aim, Fire process, I know you'll be successful in launching your business or breathing some new energy into your existing enterprise. Bottom line: the goal is to get you more speaking engagements at higher fees!

Throughout *The Wealthy Speaker*, you'll find references to this workbook. You can either read the book cover to cover first and then go back to the workbook exercises, or you can do them as you go — your choice! But make sure you have your book handy as you go through the process — it will be an invaluable reference.

Once you're finished, be sure to stay in touch with me and if you need more coaching help, I'll be standing by!

Jane Atkinson

Jane Atkinson,
Creator, The Wealthy Speaker System

❶

THE WEALTHY SPEAKER PREMISE

So What Exactly is a Wealthy Speaker?

Success is subjective. One speaker's successful year might not appeal to another speaker at all. So it's up to you to decide what success looks like for you. You might only want to speak once a month at a fee of $15,000 or you might want to speak ten times per month at $1,500. Every speaker has his or her own set of goals and no one can dictate your goals but you. What I can do, as your coach, is make sure that you are thinking big.

Stepping Up

It takes courage to move into this business from any other profession. There is a huge learning curve, not a lot of security, and you must have a higher than average level of confidence. But are you going to let fear get in your way? Turn to Coaching Exercise 1 to determine if you are ready to become a speaker. If this quiz *scares the pants off you, good*! You need to do more work before you start or perhaps you might re-evaluate.

Coaching Exercise 1: Start-Up Speaker's Quiz

Starting up a speaking business is the same as starting any business. So you must do your homework and prepare.

Ask yourself the following questions and answer with complete honesty. After all, if you can't be honest with yourself, who can you be honest with?

1. Have I done my research? What do I know about this business? What do I need to learn?

2. Is there a demand for what I offer? How many speakers are making a living doing something similar?

3. How much cash do I have set aside to launch my business?

4. Can I support a negative cash flow? For how many months?

5. Is this really what I want? Why? Am I ready now?

6. Is my speech prepared? Do I know the return on investment for the audience?

7. Is my family willing to support this?

8. How am I, or how is my message, different from that of my competition?

9. Do I know who my competition is?

10. Am I good enough to go the distance? Have people from within the industry (and people who could hire me) told me that?

11. Am I an entrepreneur? Do I know how to run a business?

12. Am I confident enough?

____

____

____

____

____

13. Do I have a solid business plan?

____

____

____

____

____

14. What will my banker and my accountant say?

____

____

____

____

____

If you answered negatively or were unsure about the majority of these questions, you might have some homework to do prior to starting this process. You might even decide that you don't want to move ahead. But if you answered positively to the majority, then we are ready to proceed. But don't think the tough questions are over – there are lots more where these came from.

For more details on this section, refer to *The Wealthy Speaker*.

Once you are ready to become a speaker, you need to define what success looks like for you. Use Coaching Exercise 2 to visualize how your life as a professional speaker will look.

When filling in the exercise "A Day in your Life Five Years from Now" think *big*! Stretch!

Coaching Exercise 2: A Day in Your Life Five Years from Now

You may want to type out this exercise and save it. We'll be referring back to it a few times. But once you're finished, you can post it somewhere prominent and look at it regularly. Olympic athletes swear by visualization exercises and, since they make it to the Olympics, I guess they must work!

Turn to page xv in *The Wealthy Speaker*, A Day in the Life of a Wealthy Speaker, for an example of a wealthy speaker's dream day. Look at the verbs used ... present tense.

Now write down what your perfect day looks like five years from now. Put down all of the details. Who do you speak for? Or consult with? At what fee? What are the results? How does that feel? What type of audience is it? What do your home and office life look like? Do you have a vacation house? Where is it? How much time do you spend there? Where else do you go for vacation? Do you have product? What are your passive income streams? What do your personal relationships look like? What kind of fun are you and your family having? Are you healthy?

Don't leave out any detail – this is your perfect day.

Once you have completed the exercise, place it in a prominent place and review it daily. Make it a part of your morning ritual. Allow the principle of "you become what you think about most of the time" to work in your favor.

**A Day in My Life
Five Years from Now**

For more details on this section, refer to *The Wealthy Speaker.*

How to Spend Your Time, Energy and Money

Throughout *The Wealthy Speaker* you will find tons of ideas for things you should be doing – from developing the speech, to building marketing materials, to setting and raising fees, to working with bureaus, to hiring staff, to setting up your office with systems, to developing product. Yikes! That could be overwhelming no matter what stage of your career you are in. Stop and take a good look at Figure A. No matter where you are in your career, you'll get some clarity around where you should best spend your time and resources. This should take off some pressure to do everything today!

Figure A: Focus Areas

New Speakers: Years 0–3	The Speech – make it good! Positioning in the market as an expert Building marketing materials that represent you (they may not be perfect) Relationships with clients – getting your name out there
Seasoned Speakers: Years 4–6	The Speech – keep working it! Getting your marketing to the next level (now it needs to be good) Building on your reputation (which means moving your fee up the ladder) Product Development – full steam ahead (some people may launch into the business with a book, and that's great too) Developing systems in your office – you'll need them now Starting to hire staff and make inroads with speakers' bureaus (work the business yourself for a few years before doing this)
Mature Speakers: Years 7+	The Speech – keep it fresh and fun for you! Reinvent it! Marketing – update (don't get complacent) Reposition if necessary – new products, new markets – stay cutting edge Continue with long-term relationship building – keep your name out there in fresh ways By now your office should run like a well oiled machine

COACH'S QUESTION: *What areas do I need to concentrate on to get my business where it needs to go?*

(Refer to *The Wealthy Speaker*, Chapter 1, under the heading How to Spend Your Time, Energy and Money, at pages 11-12.)

Notes

Notes

2

GETTING READY TO LAUNCH

COACH'S QUESTION: *Why do I want to be a speaker? What is really motivating this career choice?*

If you answer, "because I have a message that I need to share" then you might have something. You might also be on the right track if you have a strong business background and/or some unique expertise that could benefit your audiences. Any number of reasons could motivate you to get into this business. However, if you were sitting in the audience one day and saw a speaker and thought, "Hey that looks cool, I think I'll give that a shot," then you might have to stop and reassess. Your passion for your expertise is what will pull you through the tough times, so if you start out with none, you'll be reading the help wanted ads at the first sign of stress. Be sure about your motivation and be committed to the long-term process.

Now, turn the page and answer these questions. (Refer to *The Wealthy Speaker,* Chapter 2, under heading My Motivation, at pages 17–20).

COACH'S QUESTION: *Why do I want to be a speaker? What is really motivating this career choice?*

COACH'S QUESTION: *At this time, my business model will look like this:*

Example: 50% keynotes, 50% training

(Refer to *The Wealthy Speaker*, Chapter 2, under the heading Speaking Versus Training, at pages 20-23.)

Taking Action

Whether you are a speaker who is just launching your career or someone who has been in the industry for years, my goal is for you to get many juicy ideas from this book. More importantly, *I want you to take action*! Whether it be changing the way you introduce yourself or an overhaul of your entire marketing program – action is the key.

Ready, Aim, Fire

Have you ever put together a marketing campaign or designed a new one sheet or promotional piece that was a total flop? I have. Have you ever blown several hundred, or several thousand, dollars on an idea that just didn't work? I have.

If you've been shooting out ideas at random, cut it out! Commit to getting ***ready***, taking ***aim*** and hitting ***fire***.

So what's the problem? You're hitting *fire* before you get *ready* and take *aim*.

You need to start at the beginning and build a foundation for your business. What is your key message? What are the benefits to your audience? Who is your target market? What marketing materials do you need to reach them? Etc. Once this foundation is in place, you will have a much stronger foundation from which to start.

Before you put any idea to the test, ask yourself the seven pertinent questions.

1. Can I afford this idea?

   ____

   ____

   ____

2. Does it fit with my overall business strategy?

   ____

   ____

   ____

3. Does it fit with my vision of my business?

   ____

   ____

   ____

4. Can I implement this idea successfully?

   ____

   ____

   ____

5. Will this idea get me closer to my goal?

____

____

____

6. What is the payoff?

____

____

____

7. Do I know of several people who have implemented this idea with good results?

____

____

____

Those are just a few basic questions for evaluating your existing ideas as well as the ones in this book. From here on, I'm going to walk you through much of the process so you won't be shooting randomly any more.

Phases of the Wealthy Speaker Process

Figure B outlines the steps that we'll take walking through the Ready, Aim, Fire process.

Figure B: The Wealthy Speaker Process

READY	PHASE I: FOCUS	What am I selling? What is my expertise? Who is going to buy this? How will I position this and create a brand?
AIM	PHASE II: MARKETING	Update or design marketing materials that reflect your positioning and brand. How do I best explain what this is and the benefits?
FIRE	PHASE III: ROLL OUT	Who is my target market and how will I reach them? What consistent actions do I need to take to build momentum?

As you move through this process, you will want to create a list of "to do" items. Use Coaching Exercise 3 to help you create your list. For more information on this section, turn to the heading Action Steps in Chapter 2 of *The Wealthy Speaker*, at pages 27-28.

COACH'S QUESTION: *What will I allow to get in my way of starting this business?*

Really examine anything that you might allow to get in your way. Is it based on fear? Or is it legit? If it's something like your child's illness, you'll obviously need to pay attention and give yourself a break for allowing the process to be derailed. But don't allow distractions, confusion, lack of time or lack of knowledge stop you. You can work through every one of those situations if you are dedicated to this goal. When you find yourself spinning your wheels, you can usually stop to see that self-sabotage – your gremlin – is at work somewhere below the surface.

Now, use the space below to explore this question for yourself. (Refer to *The Wealthy Speaker,* Chapter 2, pages 17–34.)

Coaching Exercise 3: Action Steps Form

In each phase of the Wealthy Speaker Process, there will be action steps – tasks that must be completed in order for you to move forward and start building momentum. The Action Item List is the "to do" list of things you don't want to forget.

You can make copies of these forms, or develop your own system, for listing the ideas on which you must act and assigning a timeline to them. If you work best using spreadsheets, then by all means develop a spreadsheet. If you want to start a binder for everything, then do that. Only you know how you work best.

What's important is that you take action in order of priority and with deadlines attached.

The next three pages provide an Action Item List for each phase in the Wealthy Speaker Process.

"By When" means by what date do you want the action step completed. You may break the book down into segments in order of their importance. For example, your "A" priority might be the speech, your "B" might be developing a brand, "C" might be your website, etc. Each phase will have several action steps. When each segment is complete, you can come back and work on the next segment.

ACTION ITEM LIST
Phase I: Ready

Action Step	Priority	By When

For more details on this section, refer to *The Wealthy Speaker*.

ACTION ITEM LIST
Phase II: Aim

Action Step	Priority	By When

For more details on this section, refer to *The Wealthy Speaker*.

ACTION ITEM LIST
Phase III: Fire

Action Step	Priority	By When

For more details on this section, refer to *The Wealthy Speaker*.

COACHING EXERCISE: Removing the Gremlin

If you have identified that you have a gremlin on your shoulder – that little voice that says "you'll never pull this off" or "are you crazy, you're not talented enough" – let's bring it to the forefront so we can deal with it.

STEP 1: What does your gremlin look like, sound like and say? (Be specific and try to envision this as a real being). It may sound hokey to you, but play along.

STEP 2: Now that you know what your gremlin looks like and sounds like, let's list a few ideas of how to deal with the gremlin when it rears it's ugly head. You might say things like "grab that little jerk off my shoulder and stomp him into the ground" and visualize yourself picking it up and tossing it out of the room, putting it in the corner with a gag on it's mouth, etc. You may also use things like your genius file (see page 3 in *The Wealthy Speaker*) to help calm these negative inner thoughts. Ideally, you should be able to combat your gremlin yourself, but have a supportive friend or fellow speaker on standby just in case.

Suggested reading, *Taming Your Gremlin* by Richard Carson.

Anti-Gremlin List

____

____

____

____

____

____

____

____

____

____

____

____

____

____

____

____

Coaching Exercise 4: Checklist for Setting Up a Speaker's Office

Here's a checklist of things you will need to get your business off the ground. Refer to the explanations in *The Wealthy Speaker* in Chapter 2, under heading The Basics: Setting Up a Speaker's Office, pages 31-33, if you need more direction.

Where necessary, add items to your Action Item List under Phase I: Ready (see Coaching Exercise 3).

___ **Speech**

___ **Branding**
___ Company Name/Logo
___ URL – name for website
___ Business Cards
___ Letterhead
___ Return Labels

___ **Office Set-Up**
___ Dedicated Phone Line
___ Fax Machine and Dedicated Fax Line
___ Mailing Station

___ **Equipment**
___ Computer
___ Accounting System Software
___ File Drawers/File Folders
___ Calendar

___ **Administration**
___ Business License
___ Tax Number
___ Business Bank Accounts

Notes

Notes

❸

PHASE I: READY

Focus on Positioning and the Speech

Phase I of the Wealthy Speaker Process enables the speaker to focus on getting ready for this new career. You must focus on which topic area will bring you the most success – that will get you to your picture of A Day in Your Life Five Years from Now (see Coaching Exercise 2). Then you'll take this decision a step further and focus on becoming a true expert in this area and position yourself as the expert. Finally, developing a killer speech is the final stage on which to focus at this phase. As in many life tasks, preparation is key and focusing on this "get ready" phase is vital in the process.

The first item up is finding your passion. I see a direct correlation between plugging into your true passion or purpose and how much income you earn. The more passion – the more revenue – and the happier you are likely to be too. Turn to Coaching Exercise 5 to uncover your true calling and focus your efforts. For more information on this section, turn to the heading The Wealthy Speaker Gets Ready in Chapter 3 of *The Wealthy Speaker*, at pages 35-37.

Coaching Exercise 5: Focus Form

A good speaker can talk on a variety of topics, but a Wealthy Speaker focuses on one topic, one expertise, one set of speech materials – or even one speech – under the same umbrella. If you want to be the recognized expert – the one that meeting planners call upon when they need a speaker on that topic – you need to bring all your skill and energy to that topic. You must pick a lane.

Review the sample below and follow the process to complete the Focus Form.

Sample

Joan is a former real estate broker who loves helping women take control of their lives. She has proven it over and over in her own life and business, and she's thought about writing a book on the topic. Joan also breeds champion quarter horses and has been asked to speak several times on that topic. And as an experienced real estate broker, she's been speaking and training for years.

Joan would like to launch a speaking career. She needs to consider what she wants to be doing in her speaking business five years from now and where her passion and purpose lie.

Notice the scores she gives herself on the Take Control of your Life speech. This speech, if she works hard on the delivery, could be the one for which she becomes known and gets paid (well) to deliver. The higher the demand, the higher her fees can go. The more enthusiastic she is about the topic and the more purposeful it feels to her, then the more contagious a response she will have in her audiences, creating more demand. Women will tell other women, "You have to hear this message!"

Focus Form: Sample

Area of Expertise	Passion/Purpose	Revenue	Vision	Credibility	Relevance	Uniqueness	Talent	TOTAL
Sales: How to Sell More Real Estate	5	8	8	7	8	6	7	49
Breeding Champion Quarter Horses	8	4	6	7	7	8	7	47
Take Control of your Life – for Women	9	8	9	9	8	8	8	59

STEP 1: Review the example to understand the process.

STEP 2: List all of your speech ideas (things you could talk about) down the left hand side.

STEP 3: Rate each of your speeches on a scale of 1 to 10 – 10 being a perfect fit with the criteria listed across the top.

Here are some questions to ask yourself when rating the criteria below:

Passion: How passionate am I about this project? Is it in line with what I'm meant to do in this world?

Revenue: Is it a high revenue generator (8) or low (2)? Who will pay to hear this message? (This one is key!)

Vision: Does it fit with my long-term business vision? Can I see myself loving this topic in five years? Is it an area into which I want to immerse myself?

Credibility: Does it fit with my background and credibility? Am I walking my talk of this topic?

Relevance: Is the message timely and relevant for the audience?

Uniqueness: Is my message or delivery unique?

Talent: Am I really great at this?

STEP 4: Add the totals across and you should see which speech makes the most sense to proceed with. This is your lane!

Focus Form

Area of Expertise	Passion/Purpose	Revenue	Vision	Credibility	Relevance	Uniqueness	Talent	TOTAL

For more details on this section, refer to *The Wealthy Speaker*.

Position in the Industry

Now that you've picked your lane, you need to focus on how you position yourself as an expert in the industry.

- How are you positioning yourself in the marketplace? As a speaker? Or as an expert?
- When I look at your website, will I see the benefits of you and your expertise?
- When clients are comparing you to your competition, is fee ever a factor? (If it's a huge factor then you are not positioning well enough as an expert.)
- Are you known for one thing? For instance, are you George Smith, the guru of time management?
- When I read your bio, can I clearly define what makes you a credible expert?
- Is it evident that by hiring you, I'll be getting someone who has vast knowledge in this arena?

Don't be the jack of all trades and the master of none … be the legitimate expert!

Stating that you are the expert isn't enough, you have to be the expert. If you are at the beginning of your speaking career you might consider Coaching Exercise 6. If you've already established your expertise, you need to let your markets know. Turn to Coaching Exercise 7 for some help.

COACH'S QUESTION: *What have I done over and over in my life and career that may help define my expertise?*

An example: as early as age ten when I delivered newspapers, I had a desire to exceed my customer's expectations.

(Refer to *The Wealthy Speaker,* Chapter 3, pages 43–47.)

Coaching Exercise 6: Becoming the Expert

What do I need to do to establish myself as an expert in my market? Your answer might come in the form of a radio show, column, articles in trade publications, writing your book, developing products and tools, serving in volunteer roles in industry associations, etc. You want to publicly link your name with the topic. This approach will add to your credibility as an expert.

Brainstorm and make your list now.

1. ______________________________
2. ______________________________
3. ______________________________
4. ______________________________
5. ______________________________
6. ______________________________
7. ______________________________
8. ______________________________
9. ______________________________
10. ______________________________
11. ______________________________
12. ______________________________

For more details on this section, refer to *The Wealthy Speaker*.

Coaching Exercise 7: Presenting Your Expertise to the Marketplace

You've picked your lane; you've established your expertise; now you need to focus on how to present this package to the marketplace. For some speakers who have been around awhile, this is the missing piece of the puzzle. So spell it out for your clients and ensure it is conveyed on all your marketing materials.

Here are some questions to help you draw out the information:

1. What are the results of my presentations?

2. What am I doing for people? Allow yourself to really explore this question to understand the full value of your expertise

3. What groups am I best in front of? Who really needs this message?

4. What is most unique about me?

5. How am I credible to speak on this topic?

6. How do I best deliver my expertise (coaching, keynotes, training)?

For more details on this section, refer to *The Wealthy Speaker*.

Flashpoint

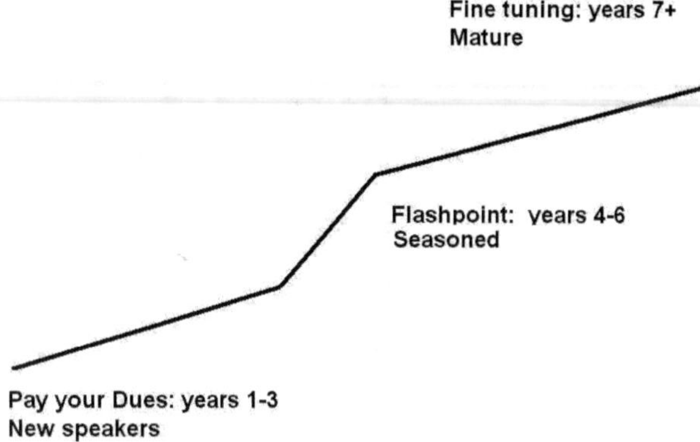

Throughout *The Wealthy Speaker* you've read Flashpoint stories. These are the points in a speakers career where they really take off. Above is the Flashpoint chart that illustrates the approximate timeline for Flashpoints. The numbers of years will vary from speaker to speaker; these are averages. And many speakers will have multiple Flashpoints throughout their careers.

Feel free to mark up this chart. Use today's date to establish your starting point and add some goal dates for when you want to be at the next stage (e.g., July 2008 mid-Flashpoint).

Components of a Great Speech

Your speech is your best marketing tool – so make sure it is great! Here are a few questions for you to think about.

- What will you say in your speech that people will remember ten years from now?
- What will you do that will impact them?
- How will you deliver your message in a unique manner?
- What phrase or common thread will hold your presentation together?
- How will you make it about them and not you?

For more details about making your speech great turn to *The Wealthy Speaker*, Chapter 3 at pages 51-65.

Bonus

COACHING EXERCISE: Industry Green Monsters

When you see another speaker – whether you admire them or not – here are a few questions to ask yourself:

What can I learn from this speaker?

___

___

What can I appreciate about their style? You don't have to change your style to be like them, but you do need to ask the question.

___

___

What is it about their style that the audiences and meeting planners love?

___

___

Why do they keep booking them? What is special about their service beyond the speech?

___

___

What do I need to do to create a buzz about my speech?

___

___

Am I being honest about my level of talent?

___

___

How can I take my speech to the next level while staying true myself?

___

___

What steps can I take to get to the Wealthy Speaker level – what is my definition of Wealthy Speaker?

___

___

What steps can I take to reach my five or ten year goals?

___

___

COACH'S QUESTION: *Am I constantly comparing myself to other speakers? How is this serving me?*

(Refer to *The Wealthy Speaker,* Chapter 3, under the heading Industry Green Monster, at pages 61–62.)

Figure C provides a big picture list of the traits of good speakers versus the traits of great speakers.

Figure C: Good Versus Great Speakers

GOOD	GREAT
Speak on many topics	Are known for one thing
Business is affected significantly by the economy	Business is steady growth consistently
Take most/all business that is offered	Accept only the business that is right for them – refer the rest to other experts
Compare themselves to others	Revel in their uniqueness and learn from people they admire
Get told they are great speakers but wish they had more business	Get two to three spin-off gigs from each engagement
Have testimonials saying they are great speakers	Have testimonials saying how the audience or the company changed as a result of their talk
Have style or substance	Have both style and substance (some exceptions apply)
Advertise in industry magazines	Are columnists in industry magazines
Buy a booth at trade shows	Are the headline keynote at trade shows
Get a standing ovation sometimes and revel in them	Don't put much stock in standing ovations whether they get them or not
Show up to give "their" speech	Make it about the audience, not themselves
May lack clarity on the value they bring	Know exactly who they are, the value they bring and walk the world with that confidence
Get asked to negotiate fees	Clients will pay what the expert charges
Business runs them	They run their business efficiently in a way that is perfect for them

COACHING EXERCISE: Speech Checklist

Use the list below to evaluate your speech and see where you might need more work.

Do Well	Needs Work	
❑	❑	I know my speech inside and out (no winging it).
❑	❑	It has a beginning, a middle and an end.
❑	❑	I use plenty of stories to illustrate my points.
❑	❑	I weave my energy throughout my presentation.
❑	❑	I set the room for success.
❑	❑	I use my voice, pitch, tone and pacing.
❑	❑	I have one central message.
❑	❑	I do my homework.
❑	❑	I use PowerPoint minimally.
❑	❑	My passion and enthusiasm shine through.
❑	❑	I know my best audience size.
❑	❑	I make it about them.
❑	❑	I am myself.
❑	❑	My introduction is solid.

Refer to Victoria LaBalme's Tip from the Masters for several more key ideas on creating a powerful presentation (see *The Wealthy Speaker* at pages 57-60).

Speaking 100+ times a year is rough on your personal life. Raise your fee and speak less!

Bonus

COACH'S QUESTION: *How many times per year can I realistically speak and lead a balanced life?*

(Refer to *The Wealthy Speaker*, Chapter 3, under the heading Side Note About Fees, at pages 70-71.)

Bonus

COACHING EXERCISE: Setting Fees

Assigning a dollar value to yourself is not an easy task. Keep in mind that a professional speaker is someone who makes a living at delivering presentations and the client is paying for two things – your unique perspective on a topic and your delivery of that perspective.

For more information about fees, see *The Wealthy Speaker*, Chapter 3, under the heading Fees – How Much Should I Charge?, at pages 66-72.

Set a BIG goal.

Take a copy of the following page and place it on your bulletin board. Remember to think big!

I will speak
_______ times per year
at a fee of
$__________.

Notes

Notes

Notes

PHASE II: AIM

Marketing to Reflect Positioning and Benefits

Taking the time in Phase I to focus on your speech and your positioning gets you *ready* to take *aim* at your marketing. Your marketing materials need to reflect the benefits of your presentation and your brand. Here I'll show you the traditional marketing components you'll need to use to promote yourself – to get your name out there.

A vital component, one that you will use throughout your marketing, is your promise statement. This is your big picture – one line – that shows the meeting planner the results of your expertise. To get to this one sentence, turn to Coaching Exercise 8.

Coaching Exercise 8: Getting to Your Promise Statement

This line explains the big picture of your bottom line results. It shows the prospective client the results of your expertise. Examples might be: "Turning Managers into Leaders", "Leading Teams Through Change", "Boosting Small Business Growth", etc.

The steps and the sample below give you an idea of the process. In the end you should have a short, powerful phrase that sums up what you do and who you do it for. Turn to the next page and create your own promise statement.

1. List all of the outcomes that take place as a result of your presentations.
2. Now that you have your list, ask the question, "If people do all of these things, what will they get?" Continue to ask until you have another list.
3. Take a look at the entire list and try to sum it up in one sentence.

Your Promise Statement: Sample

Barbara speaks to managers about building their teams. So she lists all of the outcomes (ROI) that will result because of her presentation:

1. Managers communicate more clearly and purposefully with their teams.
2. Managers will hire, develop and retain high performers.
3. Managers will make better decisions more quickly.
4. Managers will take on higher levels of responsibility in the company.

Now she looks at this list. If managers do all of the above, what will that give them? She could bat this around for awhile, but one idea would be that managers lead better. Therefore the phrase might be "Moving from Manager to Leader".

Then she needs to check in with the market place. She needs to ask clients (preferably executives), "How would your company be different if all managers were better leaders?" If they respond, "That would be fantastic", then she knows she is onto something.

Your Promise Statement

1. List all of the outcomes that take place as a result of your presentations. What will change in the organization or individual as a result of being in your session?

2. Now that you have your list, ask the question, "If people do all of these things, what will they get?" Continue to ask until you have another list.

3. Take a look at the entire list and try to sum it up in one sentence. Make sure that your promise statement is one that will appeal to meeting planners — something that makes them say, "Yes, we need that!"

For more details on this section, refer to *The Wealthy Speaker*.

To market effectively, you want to aim at three components.

- Website
- Print Materials
- Demo Video

Your Website

There are three main areas to consider when building or updating a website:

1. **Image/Marketing** – Make sure your website produces the desired image and establishes you as an expert in your field.
2. **Traffic** – This includes not just getting people there, but making them a part of your community or orbit once they arrive.
3. **Conversion** – Get them to buy a product or a service once they have visited.

Your website is your first line of offence when it comes to marketing. It's your image, it's your giant calling card, it's a chance to really Wow! the client.

Refer to *The Wealthy* Speaker, Chapter 4, under the heading Your Website at pages 85-90 for information on setting up your site, including tips on what to include and what to omit from your site. Then turn to Coaching Exercise 9 to assess your website.

COACH'S QUESTION: *How is my website unique? What can I do to separate myself from the pack?*

(Refer to *The Wealthy Speaker*, Chapter 4, under the heading Your Website, at pages 85-90.)

Coaching Exercise 9: Website Rating Form

Now that your site is built, step back and evaluate it. Try to put yourself in your client's position and look at things objectively. You may want to run a beta test and get some input from people you trust.

Rate yourself on a scale of 1 to 10 — 10 being perfect.
Many of these items will be found on your home page, but this references your entire website.

____ First Impression – does my website look professional?

____ Can the client easily determine what it is I do? Or do they have to dig?

____ Are the benefits listed?

____ Is my promise statement front and center?

____ Is my photography reflective of who I am? Is it creative or the same as every other speakers'?

____ Does my mini-bio make it clear why I am the expert to speak on this topic?

____ Do I ask a powerful question or offer a quiz that helps people see why they might need my services?

____ Are my testimonials strong enough? Do they answer the question: "What changed as a result of my services?"

____ Is my client list impressive?

____ Do I describe my uniqueness and my delivery style clearly?

____ Does the site reflect my personality, my values and my essence?

____ Do I capture names and email addresses effectively?

____ Do I have a strong call to action?

____ Is it simple for clients to get in touch with me?

Anything you rated six or less will need work in the future. Plan ahead and make the changes in stages if you feel overwhelmed. Go back and review the website section again (*The Wealthy Speaker*, pages 85-90) if you need more direction on any of these items.

For more details on this section, refer to *The Wealthy Speaker.*

Print Materials

Unless you are a graphic designer by trade, you will want to hire an expert when it comes to establishing the look of your print materials. If you are just starting out, here is your list of items from which to choose.

1. Business cards
2. Letterhead
3. One sheet
4. Template page
5. Folder
6. Stickers for folder, video, etc.

Bonus

COACHING EXERCISE: One Sheet Checklist

The one sheet is used to present an image to the client, give them some information about you and establish your area of expertise. The following are the components for your one sheet, should you choose to create one.

Refer to *The Wealthy Speaker*, Chapter 4, at pages 92-95, for further details.

- ❑ Your name and what you do – remember: expert first, speaker second
- ❑ Photo of you
- ❑ Photo of your book
- ❑ Promise statement
- ❑ Brief paragraph that backs up promise statement
- ❑ Brief paragraph that describes your credibility (mini-bio)
- ❑ Program titles and mini-outlines with ROI bullets
- ❑ Client testimonials and mini-client list
- ❑ Quote from you – something that grabs their attention

Demo Video

Unlike websites and print materials that are mostly for image, the main use of your demo video is to secure bookings. It should stand alone without any other marketing materials and needs to establish who you are and your area of expertise. It should demonstrate enough of your live speaking presentation to answer the question: "Why should I hire this speaker over all of the others?"

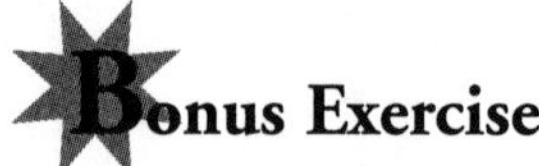

Bonus Exercise

COACHING EXERCISE: Killer Video Checklist

Your Demo Video will become the deciding factor for speakers' bureaus and event organizers. Use the checklist to make sure your video rocks!

Refer to *The Wealthy Speaker*, Chapter 4, at pages 95-104, for further details.

Yes	No	
❑	❑	Are the first 45 seconds awesome?
❑	❑	Am I speaking within the first minute?
❑	❑	Does it have humor?
❑	❑	Is it up front?
❑	❑	Does it showcase my storytelling?
❑	❑	Does it have good energy?
❑	❑	Is the production quality high?
❑	❑	Is the audience reacting (laughing, engaged)?
❑	❑	Are they with me?
❑	❑	Is it brief?
❑	❑	Can the client clearly see my benefits and ROI?
❑	❑	Is it easy to see how I help people (big picture)?
❑	❑	Does it demonstrate my expertise?
❑	❑	Does it show the client why I am credible to deliver this message?
❑	❑	Does it showcase my style?
❑	❑	Does it answer the question "why should I hire this speaker"?

Remember to test your video before sending it out *en mass*.

Notes

Notes

5

PHASE III: FIRE

Rolling Out to Your Market

If you think making your speech great, positioning yourself as an expert and developing the appropriate marketing materials was tough, you need to take a deep breath. You've only just started. Now you need to identify your target market and determine the best method to reach them. You need to roll out your product and continue to build momentum. You're *ready*, you've taken *aim*, now *fire*!

COACH'S QUESTION: *What methods have you used to get your name, message and expertise out to your target market and potential audiences?*

If you've been letting the local media know that you are presenting a speech at the local merchant's group – good for you. If you've written a press release about the decline in sales in downtown shops due to the big box mall on the edge of town – better for you. If you've been submitting a monthly column in the local paper about retailing – best for you. Whether it be writing articles for your industry magazine or getting a slot on CNN, getting press can help set you up as the expert.

(Refer to *The Wealthy Speaker*, Chapter 5, under the heading Public Relations, at pages 105-117.)

COACHING EXERCISE: Hiring an Agency or Publicist

Self-promotion is not easy for most people and it is a full-time job in and of itself. Hiring an agency or publicist can lighten your load. Some of the things you'll want to consider before hiring someone to help you promote yourself or your book are listed below.

1. Do they know my market?

   ____
   ____
   ____

2. Do they understand my goals?

   ____
   ____
   ____

3. Do they have the contacts that I need?

   ____
   ____
   ____

4. Do they have a good reputation?

   ____
   ____
   ____

5. What is their track record?

   ____
   ____
   ____

6. Will they work hard for me or will I get lost in the pile?

   ____
   ____
   ____

7. Who has used them with success? Try to find some of your own references as well as the ones they provide. Ask them for at least six people, then call the bottom of the list first.

   ____
   ____
   ____

8. Are they based in the middle of the marketplace? For example if you are hiring a literary agent, you most likely want someone based out of New York, so that they are constantly in the thick of the business. Face-to-face relationships are often the most powerful and they would have the edge on literary agents located elsewhere.

___

___

___

9. If possible, go to their offices and see how organized they are – if it's mayhem, then you may reconsider.

___

___

___

10. Will I have to sign a long-term contract? If so, then think very carefully. Many speakers have been completely dissatisfied with their PR firms, so make sure you have a trial period before locking into anything long term. Or better yet, use an agency on a project basis.

___

___

___

Finding Business

The first step in attracting the customers that you desire is getting very clear on identifying your perfect customer. I would break that down even further to define who your perfect audience is as well. Coaching Exercise 10 will help you identify that perfect customer and audience.

Coaching Exercise 10: Qualities of Your Perfect Customer

The first step is getting very clear on identifying your perfect customer. If you are just starting out in the speaking industry, you will need to go out and speak a lot before you will really know who is perfect for you. You might have to do a lot of speaking engagements that are not right for you, before you can see clearly who is the best, most perfect audience.

Your Perfect Customer: Sample

You've been speaking professionally for six months and have been told by several people that you are really good. So you start to draft your perfect customer list. You write that your perfect client has audiences of more than 5,000 people and they are all CEOs.

If in your seventh month of speaking, you speak to this audience, you could be making a huge career blunder. The reason? Unless you are freakishly talented, the odds are that you aren't ready for this group. It may take two or three years to be able to handle a group of that size and stature and it's important that you ensure you are ready before you get in front of them. You might start with groups of 50-100 CEOs and work your way up.

Your Perfect Customer

List the qualities of your perfect customer (including what their audience might look like).

1. ______
2. ______
3. ______
4. ______
5. ______
6. ______
7. ______
8. ______
9. ______
10. ______
11. ______
12. ______
13. ______
14. ______
15. ______
16. ______
17. ______
18. ______
19. ______
20. ______
21. ______
22. ______
23. ______
24. ______
25. ______

I would highly recommend walking through all of the steps in the book *Attracting Your Perfect Customer.*

For more details on this section, refer to *The Wealthy Speaker.*

For a designated period of time, say six months, speak wherever they will listen.

Bonus

COACH'S QUESTION: *List the companies or associations you might approach to offer your speech for free.*

(Refer to *The Wealthy Speaker*, Chapter 5, under heading, Speak Wherever They Will Listen, at page 115.)

____

____

____

____

____

____

____

____

____

____

____

____

____

____

____

____

____

Rolling Out to Your Market

Now you come to the nitty-gritty. It's time to put everything together and book those engagements.

When you are preparing to make your phone calls or send query emails you want to be wearing your attraction hat rather than your sales hat. When you are picking up the phone it should be to see whether or not the client has a need that your services match. Get yourself into attraction or matching mode by thinking about the value that you have to offer (you are the expert) before picking up the phone. Coaching Exercise 11, The Value You Offer, can help keep you focused when making calls.

Coaching Exercise 11: The Value You Offer

List the value that you bring to an organization. Organize your list and print it out in bullet form and post it in front of you before picking up the phone to make "matching" calls. Remember when you are talking to prospective clients to give them stories that they can "hang their hat on".

The Value I Offer: Sample

1. I provide a strategy for increasing sales.
2. My strategy covers three areas that are integral to selling success: authenticity, integrity and value.
3. My average clients ROI is a 25% increase in customer loyalty.
4. My client, ABC company, used these techniques to close two $50,000 deals within a one-week period.

The Value I Offer

____

____

____

____

____

____

____

____

____

____

____

____

____

____

____

____

____

____

____

____

____

For more details on this section, refer to *The Wealthy Speaker*.

Who to Call

Being specific about your target market or focus is always the way to go. That doesn't mean you won't try some things that will fail and then move on to new ideas, but you want to be focused in your tests.

Bonus

COACHING EXERCISE: Choosing Target Market Criteria

Choose your target market that matches the following criteria:

1. What industries need your message?

2. What industries can afford you?

3. What industries have enough business to keep you speaking for several years?

4. What groups of people are you passionate about and enjoy presenting to?

Cold Calling – Questions to Ask

Here are a list of questions to keep handy when making cold calls. Make a copy and pin it up by your phone.

- Are you the person who is in charge of booking the speakers for your upcoming conferences? If not, who?
- When is your next event?
- When will you be planning for this event? If they say six months from now, try to gain more information about the event and schedule a time to call back.
- How many paid speakers will you book for this event? "Paid" is the key word. If this association doesn't pay its speakers, then move on.
- How is the decision made? By one person? Who? By committee?
- What topics will you want to include in this year's conference? Ask if your topic would be of interest to this audience. Make sure you state the benefits of the speech.
- What is your budget for each speaker? Breakout? Keynote? Ask about your specific slot.
- In what city will the event be held? You should know this ahead of time.
- How many people will attend?
- What is the demographic? What job(s) do they do?
- What is your theme? This is your opportunity to talk about how your speech would fit. Keep asking questions about the group's needs to keep his or her interest. You may even suggest he or she go to your website while on the line with you.
- Who did you have speaking last year? Try to know this ahead of time as well and be prepared to discuss how you might follow up with that speaker.
- When will you make the decision regarding speakers?
- May I send you materials? Which format suits best – web, email, mail, video, DVD, CD?
- When will you be reviewing my materials?
- When should I get back in touch? How? Phone, email?

COACH'S QUESTION: *What can I say to prospects on the phone that will result in gaining their interest? What will make us "click"?*

Do your research. Bring up specific details about the company, such as what is on the website. You also need to listen carefully and respond to the needs they express. Don't forget to mention your value/benefits, but phrase it in terms of their needs. Make it about them. For instance, you might say, "Joanne, when I was studying your association's website, I noticed that you had a lot of sales training scheduled throughout the year for your people. Would a program that could help them build 25% more customer loyalty be helpful to your audience?"

(Refer to *The Wealthy Speaker*, Chapter 5, at pages 126-127.)

Building a Database

From day one of your business, you should be adding names to a database and putting them into categories. Are they "speaking prospects", "product prospects", "friends", etc. You may want to categorize your clients by year (2006 Keynote Client) so it's easy to pull them all up at the end of the year to recap or to send holiday greetings.

Here is some of the information for which you will want to set up fields.

- Organization (this and all of the standard info like address, etc., is already set up)
- Contact Name (if there are multiple meeting planners, you can easily set up a group)
- Date of Next Meeting (make sure that you put it in a format that you can easily search)
- Location of Next Meeting (what city)
- Planning Month (when will they be doing their planning)
- Number of Speakers (they use at their event)
- Fee Quoted
- Industry Type (you may want to set this up as a drop down list, again for easy searching)

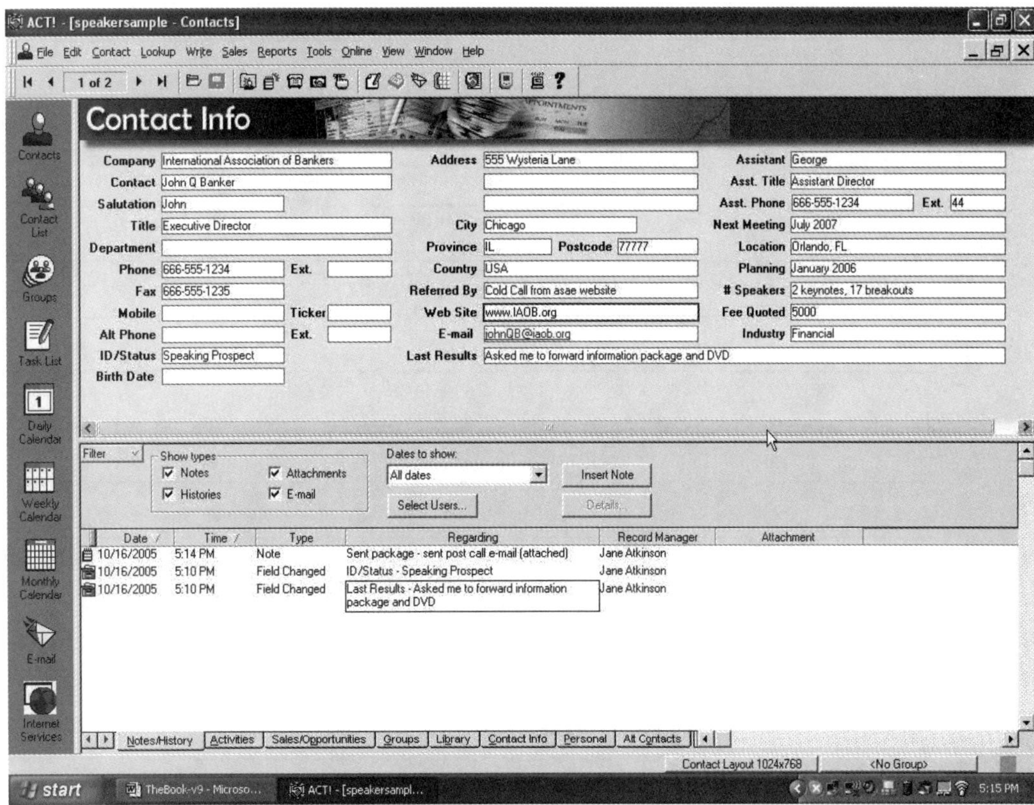

Reprinted with permission of Sage Software SB, Inc. All rights reserved. The Sage Software logo and ACT! are registered trademarks or trademarks of Sage Software SB, Inc. or its affiliated entities.

COACH'S QUESTION: *What methods will I use to build my database?*

(Refer to *The Wealthy Speaker*, Chapter 5, under heading, Database Building Strategies, at pages 133-138.)

Bonus

COACH'S QUESTION: *What methods will I use to lead people to my website?*

(Refer to *The Wealthy Speaker*, Chapter 5, under heading, All Roads Lead to Your Website, at pages 137-138.)

Flow of the Booking

Every time you book an engagement, a series of things should fall into place. Consistency is key so develop a system with a checklist and stick to it.

Bonus

COACHING EXERCISE: Booking Checklist

Client Folder

❑ Create Folder

❑ Create Label: Client name:

Date of Engagement: ____________________

City: ____________________

❑ Print additional Labels

Agreement

❑ Create Document

❑ Send to Client

❑ Enclosures to Client

❑ Copy in your Client Folder

❑ Notes on Calendar

Contact Management

❑ Tag Client info in software

Event Details Form

❑ Client Details

❑ Event Details

❑ Travel Details: Flight ____________________

Ground ____________________

Hotel ____________________

Misc. ____________________

Expenses Envelope

❑ Attach Client Label

❑ Place in Client Folder

Handouts

❑ Place originals in Client Folder

❑ Include Additional Items:

___ Leads Baggies/Envelope

___ Thank-you Cards

___ Extra Labels

COACH'S QUESTION: *What will I do to make the most of every speaking engagement?*

(Refer to *The Wealthy Speaker*, Chapter 5, under heading, Making the Most of Each Speaking Engagement, at pages 141-143.)

COACH'S QUESTION: *How many opportunities (for speeches, consulting, training or coaching) did I let slip through my fingers because I was focused on closing one speech?*

Did you follow up on all the leads you received after your gig or have they cooled off? Did you spend enough time investigating the training opportunities with that fellow from Nortel? Have you followed up on that successful gig with the Missouri Bankers and asked for a referral for their national conference?

(Refer to *The Wealthy Speaker*, Chapter 5, under the heading Making the Most of Each Speaking Engagement, at pages 141-144.)

Notes

Notes

6

SPEAKERS' BUREAUS AND EVENT PLANNING COMPANIES

Now that you have been booking your gigs on your own for a few years, you might want to enlist the help of our industry's intermediaries. These are the companies that help corporate and association meeting planners put together their events.

There are many different types of agencies. A client may use a *destination management* (DM) company to help with the location. Or they may hire an *event planner* to deal with everything from speakers to table settings. A *production company* may step in to do the staging and all of the audio visual components. These companies may have an in-house speakers' bureau or they may work with speakers' bureaus.

Are You Ready?

Most speakers' bureaus (with rare exceptions) are not going to launch a speaker's career. They will most likely start paying attention to you after you have built a name for yourself.

Bonus

COACHING EXERCISE: Are You Ready for Bureaus?

To see if you are ready to work with bureaus, ask yourself the following questions:

Yes	No	
❑	❑	Have I given 30 or more paid speeches per year for at least two years?
❑	❑	Is my fee high enough? $3,500 is an average minimum, but some bureaus require $5,000.
❑	❑	Are my materials ready (demo video, one sheets, etc.) and do they sell me?
❑	❑	Am I really good? Am I getting two or three spin-off engagements from each speech?

If you answered "yes" to all these questions, you are ready.

If a bureau has placed you on hold more than ten times without a booking, there could be two issues at hand: they don't know exactly how to position and sell you or your video is not competing in the marketplace. If it's the latter, then you will hear this from more than one bureau and know that your video (and possibly your speech) needs some work. If it's the former, then you might ask if you can spend 15 minutes on the phone with the sales team to help improve the closing ratio. Coaching Exercise 12 will help you develop a quick and easy sheet to which speakers' bureau agents can refer. For more information on working with speakers' bureaus, turn to *The Wealthy Speaker*, Chapter 6, at pages 146-155.

Coaching Exercise 12: Positioning Page

It's a very common issue for bureaus not to understand what a speaker does. Make sure your marketing materials are doing their job and use this exercise to provide the bureau with a clear understanding of how to sell you.

The first column represents the speakers' bureaus questions and requirements. The second column provides the bureau with the answers so they will "get" you and, in turn, be able to sell you.

Look at the Sam Seaborn example as a template.

Then, fill in the Positioning Page according to your business. This form may be used for in-house purposes, as well as for bureaus. Notice how the language in the sample is kept to a minimum – it's sparse and gives them just what they need. If you turn this form into three or four pages, you will lose the interest of bureau agents.

Sample Bureau Positioning Page: Sam Seaborn

When should I submit Sam for a program?	When the client is seeking a high energy speaker on the topic of motivation or peak performance. When a client wants to breathe some life into their organization.
Best Audience:	Sam works extremely well with sales teams.
What is Sam best known for?	Sam's book "The Seaborn System: Six Keys to Achieving Everything You Want" is a national bestseller.
What topics should Sam be listed under in our database?	Motivation, inspiration, sales, peak performance, sports/athletes
What is most unique about Sam?	Sam's system was developed while he trained to compete in his first Iron Man triathlon. What made it more unique was that Sam was also recovering from a nearly fatal heart attack at age 35.
What parallels does Sam draw for a business audience, i.e., how does it relate to them?	Prior to his heart attack Sam was #1 in sales at ABC company. He was like so many people in the audience who were focused on the wrong goals.
When does Sam shine the brightest?	Sam is best at opening an event with extremely high energy that will last throughout the entire meeting.
When would Sam not be the best fit?	Sam does not fit during an after dinner (with alcohol) program.
What are the results of Sam's presentations? What do clients comment most about?	Once employees apply The Seaborn System, they will improve their performance by up to 40% and they will lead balanced and more productive, happier lives.
What is the best sales/closing strategy for booking Sam?	Sam's video consistently works to close business, but a phone call with Sam and the client can speed the booking along more quickly. Once the client speaks with Sam – it's a done deal.
Who is Sam most similar to?	Although he is different from them, Sam often shares the platform with people like Keith Harrell, Vince Poscente, Amanda Gore and Mark Sanborn.

POSITIONING PAGE: ______________________ **DATE:** ______________

When should I submit (your name here) for a program?	
Best Audience:	
What is _______ best known for?	
What topics should _______ be listed under in our database?	
What is most unique about ____________?	
What parallels does _______ draw for a business audience, i.e., how does it relate to them?	
When does ______________ shine the brightest?	
When would ______________ not be the best fit?	
What are the results of _______'s presentations? What do clients comment most about?	
What is the best sales/ closing strategy for booking ________?	
Who is _________ most similar to?	

For more details on this section, refer to *The Wealthy Speaker*.

Notes

GROWING YOUR BUSINESS BEYOND GIGS

Look back to Coaching Exercise 2. Does your typical day look like Your Day Five Years from Now? Or will it in the near future? If you answer "yes", congratulations. You've accomplished a feat many people never do. If you answer "no", we need to discover why not. Perhaps you want to grow your business further. You could develop products and diversify your business or you could hire staff to take care of the business so you can focus on your speech and satisfy your clients' needs.

Developing Product

Products can be used as a promotional tool or to lend credibility and be a concrete example of your expertise. They can form a small or big part of your business. The type of products you offer may vary with your area of expertise, but some of the typical products are:

- Books
- Audio
- Video/DVD
- Bundling.

If you walk around NSA long enough, you'll hear it said that you must write a book in order to establish expertise. I wasn't sure if I believed that in the early days, but now I do. When a speaker doesn't have a book, I ask "why".

Before you decide how to publish your book, get clear on the type of book you want.

Bonus

COACHING EXERCISE: Do You Have a Book Inside You?

What type of book do you want to create?

____

____

Who will buy this book?

____

____

What is the main purpose of the book?

____

____

Who will I need to help me?

____

____

How will I sell this book?

____

____

____

Refer to the Publishing Quiz in Coaching Exercise 13 on the next page for more clarity on this topic.

Coaching Exercise 13: Publishing Quiz

Before you decide how to publish your book, get clear on the type of book you want. A souvenir book is a product that you sell at the back of the room when your audience simply wants to take a piece of you home with them. Expert books help to establish serious credibility in the marketplace and appeal to a broader range of readers. Take the quiz to see which route is perfect for you.

Keep three considerations in mind when deciding which way to publish your book: time; credibility; and profit. Complete both quizzes to determine which method will work for you.

Quiz One – Expert Book

Yes	No	
☐	☐	Do I want to be nationally recognized as a leading expert in my field?
☐	☐	Do I want to sell my books all over the world?
☐	☐	Do I want to have a shot at writing a bestseller?
☐	☐	I do not care how long it takes to publish my book?
☐	☐	I do not care how much money I make on my book?
☐	☐	I do not care if I have to give up some of the creative control on my book?

Quiz Two – Souvenir Book

Yes	No	
☐	☐	Do I want my clients and prospects to see me as credible?
☐	☐	Do I want to have something to sell at my speeches?
☐	☐	My first priority is not getting my book in stores?
☐	☐	Do I want to make a lot of money from my book?
☐	☐	Do I want my book to be published quickly?
☐	☐	Do I want 100% creative control over the process?

If you answered most of the questions in Quiz One with "yes", then finding a publisher is probably the way to go. If you answered mostly "yes" in Quiz Two, then you are probably better suited to self-publishing. There is more prestige in going with a publisher, but the odds of a publisher picking up your book are relatively low. A bestselling book could be the difference between a $5,000 keynote fee and a $25,000 fee, but again, the odds are not stacked in your favor. Clients may see a big name publisher as more credible than self-publishing, but you have to weigh all of the pros and cons and look at your goals. Finding a literary agent and writing a book proposal can take eight to twelve months. You don't always need a lit agent to get a publisher. Remember: you still have to write the book!

For more details on this section, refer to *The Wealthy Speaker*.

COACHING EXERCISE: Bundling

Here are some things for you to think about when bundling products.

What is the best way to offer value to my clients — in a package or system?

What products can I develop that compliment each other (i.e., book, video, audio combo)?

What can I offer of my time to increase the value of my products?

How can I develop bundles that all have a theme (i.e., sales bundle, time management bundle, etc.)?

Is there someone that I can partner with on a product to add to my bundle?

Is there a product that I can purchase to add to my bundle to increase its value (i.e., poster, promotional product, calendar, etc.)?

What products could I produce that no one has ever thought of?

Bonus

COACH'S QUESTION: *What other products do I wish to develop? (e.g., audio, video, promotional products, posters, mugs, etc.).*

(Refer to *The Wealthy Speaker*, Chapter 7, under the heading Developing Product, at pages 165-178.)

Hiring Staff Who are Winners

With a few exceptions, most of the Wealthy Speakers in the field (top 3%) have a great marketing person or team behind them. Tony Alessandra had Holli Catchpole (who was my idol when I first started in the industry), Larry Winget has Vic Osteen and Amanda Gore had Somer McCormick and now works with Holli Catchpole (how's that for a small world). How these people came together in the first place probably took some luck or synchronicity, but you want to do your best to hedge your bets when finding that perfect marketing person.

The hiring process has five steps:

1. Are you ready to hire?
2. What should this person do for you?
3. How much should you pay?
4. Who is the right fit?
5. Where will you find them?

Bonus

COACHING EXERCISE: Ready to Hire?

Here are a few questions to determine whether you are ready to hire a marketing person to help build your speaking business.

Yes	No	
❑	❑	Are you losing business because you don't have time (or desire) to fill your business pipeline or follow up leads?
❑	❑	Have you worked the business yourself for at least a year and know how to get bookings? Can you train someone else to do this?
❑	❑	Can you afford to pay a base salary plus commission? Most good marketing people will not work for straight commission.
❑	❑	Can you afford to make a mistake in hiring or will a bad choice put your business in jeopardy?

If you can answer "yes" to most of these questions then you are ready to take the next step. Coaching Exercise 14 will help you develop a job description for your assistant. Then all you have to do is find and hire someone that meets that criteria. You'll find more information on this topic in Chapter 7 of *The Wealthy Speaker*, under the heading Hiring Staff Who Are Winners, at pages 178-186.

Coaching Exercise 14: Developing a Job Description

One of the biggest mistakes speakers make when hiring is not getting clear on their needs until after they have hired. You need to be clear on what tasks you want this person to perform for you. Do you want someone to do the $10/hour jobs? Or someone to do outbound marketing? Do you want someone to pick up your dry cleaning? Or are you looking for a combination?

Use the list of tasks to determine what your assistant should do. The lists are broken down into categories: getting speaking engagements; administrative duties; and personal assistant. At the end of the exercise you will have the basis for a job description.

Get Speaking Engagements	**Administrative Duties**	**Personal Assistant**
❑ Prospecting	❑ Booking travel	❑ Picking up dry cleaning
❑ Cold calling/telemarketing	❑ Generating invoices/ bookkeeping	❑ Feeding the fish
❑ Marketing to and working with bureaus	❑ Schedule management	❑ Keeping you organized
❑ Developing or updating marketing materials	❑ Gig logistics	❑ Arranging for baby sitters
❑ Proposal writing	❑ Product fulfillment (shipping)	❑ Arranging family trips, etc.
❑ Sending out marketing materials or email	❑ Database management	
❑ Proposals (designing, sending out)	❑ Newsletter management	
❑ Closing deals (overcoming objections, etc.)	❑ Web site management	
❑ Meeting with clients	❑ Managing other business' interests/investments, etc.	
❑ Mass marketing – mailings or emails		
❑ Showcase events		
❑ Following up leads from gigs		
❑ New product development		

For more details on this section, refer to *The Wealthy Speaker*.

Bonus

COACH'S QUESTION: *What traits will my perfect staff person possess? How will I find this person?*

(Refer to *The Wealthy Speaker*, Chapter 7, under heading, Hiring Staff Who are Winners, at pages 178-186.)

Agreements and Contracts

New speakers can skip over the checklist in Coaching Exercise 15 and come back to it later when needed. Your agreements can be fairly basic in the beginning. However, as your business grows, contracts become more necessary for both you and your client. (Refer to *The Wealthy Speaker*, Chapter 7, under the heading Agreements and Contracts, at pages 186-195, for more details.)

Coaching Exercise 15: Agreement and Contract Checklist

Your agreements should be thorough without being a pain in the butt for the meeting planner. You want your agreement to stick, you want your clients to understand all of the money details and what happens if they cancel, but, at the same time, you don't want to scare them off.

Below is a list of items that should be included in every agreement and contract. Please refer to *The Wealthy Speaker* at pages 186–195 for more information. A sample agreement is on the next page.

- ❑ Your Name
- ❑ Date of the Agreement
- ❑ Client's Company or Group Name
- ❑ Client's Contact Information
- ❑ Event Date
- ❑ Speech Start Time and Finish Time
- ❑ Other Time Requirements
- ❑ Title of Presentation
- ❑ Speaking Fee
- ❑ Cancellation Policy
- ❑ Venue Address, Phone, Fax
- ❑ Introducer's Name
- ❑ Audio/Video Taping Release
- ❑ Air Travel
- ❑ Hotel Address, Phone and Fax Numbers (if different from speaking venue)
- ❑ Ground Transportation
- ❑ AV Requirements
- ❑ Handouts/Support Materials

Sample Agreement

logo

Speaker Agreement – Jon Duncan

CLIENT INFORMATION:

Contact Person: Fontana James
Title: VP of Sales
Organization: ITMB Staffing
Address: 1444 Garland Rd., Dallas, TX 75226
Phone: 214-555-5552 **Fax:** 214-555-5551 **Email:** fontanaj@ITMB.com

TITLE OF PRESENTATION/WORKSHOP: Secrets of the Staffing Wizards
DATE OF PRESENTATION/WORKSHOP: January 21, 2007
TIME OF PRESENTATION/WORKSHOP: 1:00pm–2:30pm (90-minute program)
LOCATION OF PRESENTATION/WORKSHOP: Hotel St. George, Roosevelt Room 555 Hotel Lane, Dallas, TX 75666

The client agrees to pay the following fees and expenses:

The fee for this presentation/workshop is: **$7,000**

A non-refundable 50% deposit of **$3,500** is due by **12/31/06** to secure the engagement date. If client cancels 45 days or less (without immediately rescheduling) the entire fee will be due as complete settlement. Should the speaker miss the engagement due to illness or emergency and a suitable replacement cannot be found, client will be reimbursed in full.

Deposit payable to: Duncan Consulting (Tax ID# 04-933333)
Address: 555 Wysteria Lane, Austin, TX 76229

The balance of **$3,500** to be handed to the speaker on engagement day.

Travel Expenses:
Expenses include full coach airfare, meals, ground transportation and lodging. These expenses will be invoiced after the program. Jon Duncan will use his best efforts to keep travel expenses to a minimum.

Support Materials:
Mr. Duncan's products, including books and tapes, may be made available for participants to purchase after his program(s), unless specified otherwise.

AV Requirements/Audio-Video Release: Wireless microphone, 6 foot table at back of room. Videotaping of Mr. Duncan's presentation is acceptable for internal use only. In return, we request a high quality master copy of the presentation.

Our signatures on this agreement indicate full compliance with the requests and the promises above, and complete understanding of the services to be provided.

______________________________ ______________________________
Client Date Speaker Date

For the entire program, turn to the fll text in *The Wealthy Speaker*.

The High Tech Speaker on the Road

I can't stress enough to beginning speakers that keeping your business simple in the early days is imperative. You can add bells and whistles with technology as you go. The majority of your income in the first few years should be spent on the speech and marketing.

COACHING EXERCISE: High Tech Tools and Shopping List

Here are the baker's dozen tools of the trade for the ultimate high tech speaker. A shopping list on the next page will help you plan and acquire these tools.

	Need Now	Need Later	Don't Need
1. Cell phone/handheld unit (BlackBerry).	❑	❑	❑
2. Digital camera built into phone or separate.	❑	❑	❑
3. Wireless Laptop.	❑	❑	❑
4. Portable printer – under 5 lbs. designed for travel.	❑	❑	❑
5. Presentation Software, if you use PowerPoint or something similar.	❑	❑	❑
6. Wireless Remote for presentation slides.	❑	❑	❑
7. Projector/Lavaliere Mic. Some speakers do carry their own.	❑	❑	❑
8. Digital Recording Device to audio record every speech.	❑	❑	❑
9. Business Card Scanner if you are constantly sending leads to speakers' bureaus.	❑	❑	❑
10. Website Management Software. Some may choose not to do this themselves.	❑	❑	❑
11. Contact Management Software.	❑	❑	❑
12. Calendar Management Software.	❑	❑	❑
13. Virtual Terminal or Swipe Terminal for product sales back of room.	❑	❑	❑

Shopping List

Item	Needed By	Done
		☐
		☐
		☐
		☐
		☐
		☐
		☐
		☐
		☐
		☐
		☐
		☐
		☐
		☐
		☐
		☐
		☐
		☐
		☐
		☐
		☐
		☐
		☐
		☐
		☐
		☐
		☐
		☐
		☐

Notes

Notes

POSTSCRIPT

You're done! Congratulations on taking the steps towards becoming a *Wealthy Speaker*.

What's next? Well, that depends.

If you've completed the Ready, Aim, Fire process and you've moved towards your target markets successfully, then you're on your way. Keep going! If you feel as though you still need some help, drop me a line at *jane@speakerlauncher.com* and we'll look at next steps with the help of coaching.

Enjoy your journey!

Jane Atkinson

Jane Atkinson,
Creator, The Wealthy Speaker System

Praise for Jane Atkinson and *The Wealthy Speaker*…

"Speakers are many but truly wealthy speakers are few. If you aspire to be a wealthy speaker—or a *wealthier* speaker—this book if for you. Jane doesn't just *know* what she writes about, she's *done* it."

— Mark Sanborn, CSP, CPAE
Author, *The Fred Factor*

"I wish I had *The Wealthy Speaker* as a roadmap when I got into this business 20 years ago … I could have saved a ton of time and money!"

— Amanda Gore, CSP
Author of *You Can Be Happy*

"Before you open your mouth to speak be sure to open Jane Atkinson's book to learn how, to whom, about what, and how much you should get paid to speak."

— Larry Thompson,
Hollywood Film Producer and Manager
Author of *SHINE: A Powerful 4-Step Formula for Being a Star at Anything You Do*

"Jane has written the definitive book on how to speak and get paid, as well as, how to fill your calendar with the right speaking engagements!"

— Mark LeBlanc
Author of *Growing Your Business!*

"What are you waiting for? *Run*, don't walk, to read this book! If you apply even one idea, you'll take a quantum leap forward in your career! There are gems for both beginner and experienced speakers alike."

— Andrea H. Gold
President, Gold Stars Speakers Bureau

"Jane is one of the true pros in the speaker marketing business. Her knowledge and experience are invaluable for anyone who strives to be a wealthy speaker."

— Vic Osteen
General Manager, WIN Seminars

"*The Wealthy Speaker* is the bible of the speaking industry. Make a date with Jane Atkinson to make your business soar. It will be the best investment you have ever made."

— Betska K-Burr, MPC Vice President,
Coaching and Leadership International Inc.

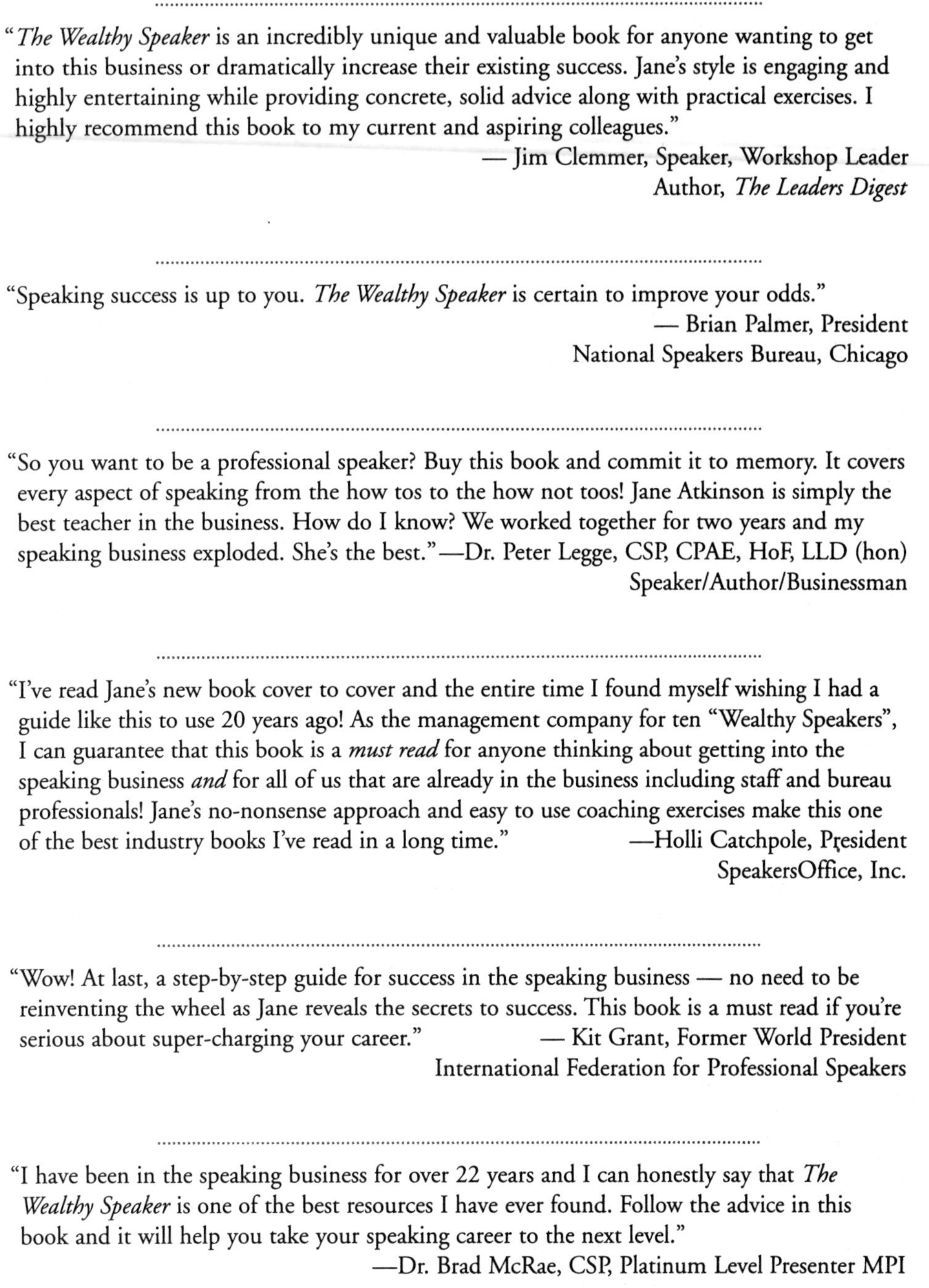

"*The Wealthy Speaker* is an incredibly unique and valuable book for anyone wanting to get into this business or dramatically increase their existing success. Jane's style is engaging and highly entertaining while providing concrete, solid advice along with practical exercises. I highly recommend this book to my current and aspiring colleagues."

— Jim Clemmer, Speaker, Workshop Leader
Author, *The Leaders Digest*

"Speaking success is up to you. *The Wealthy Speaker* is certain to improve your odds."

— Brian Palmer, President
National Speakers Bureau, Chicago

"So you want to be a professional speaker? Buy this book and commit it to memory. It covers every aspect of speaking from the how tos to the how not toos! Jane Atkinson is simply the best teacher in the business. How do I know? We worked together for two years and my speaking business exploded. She's the best."—Dr. Peter Legge, CSP, CPAE, HoF, LLD (hon)
Speaker/Author/Businessman

"I've read Jane's new book cover to cover and the entire time I found myself wishing I had a guide like this to use 20 years ago! As the management company for ten "Wealthy Speakers", I can guarantee that this book is a *must read* for anyone thinking about getting into the speaking business *and* for all of us that are already in the business including staff and bureau professionals! Jane's no-nonsense approach and easy to use coaching exercises make this one of the best industry books I've read in a long time."

—Holli Catchpole, President
SpeakersOffice, Inc.

"Wow! At last, a step-by-step guide for success in the speaking business — no need to be reinventing the wheel as Jane reveals the secrets to success. This book is a must read if you're serious about super-charging your career."

— Kit Grant, Former World President
International Federation for Professional Speakers

"I have been in the speaking business for over 22 years and I can honestly say that *The Wealthy Speaker* is one of the best resources I have ever found. Follow the advice in this book and it will help you take your speaking career to the next level."

—Dr. Brad McRae, CSP, Platinum Level Presenter MPI